Scrizzie Deals With Honesty

By Let A Kid Help LLC

Illustrations by Chris Miller

xulon PRESS

Scrizzie Deals With Honesty
by Let A Kid Help LLC

Printed in the United States of America

ISBN 9781619963917

www.xulonpress.com

Scrizzie's mom walked up the stairs to his room. "Are you getting ready for school, Scrizzie?" she called out. "I hope you're up and preparing for your day."

Do you think Scrizzie was up and at 'em as his mom hoped? Oh , no. Instead Scrizzie lay snuggled beneath his favorite blue blanket, all warm and cozy. He was dreaming and did not want it to end. Scrizzie was dreaming about a place called Thankfulville.Thankfulville was a beautiful land far beyond the clouds, where everything could talk, including the clouds! In Thankfulville everyone was thankful for who they were and what they had.

THANKFULVILLE

There were oodles and oodles of clouds in Thankfulville. In fact, every little boy and girl was assigned his or her own special cloud. Scrizzie was assigned to a clever little cloud named Zoomy. Zoomy was smart and very fast.

Scrizzie and Zoomy were zipping along through the bright, blue sky when suddenly a strong wind named Gust came whirling by.

"Hey, watch it!"

Scrizzie and Zoomy were shaken all about. Scrizzie held onto his blanket tightly as the shaking became stronger.

Scrizzie tossed and turned. His dream felt so real he could actually hear Zoomy calling his name. "SSccrriizzzziiee!" The shaking increased. Scrizzie opened his eyes one at a time. His vision was a little blurry, but he recognized his mother standing over him.

"Scrizzie, wake up! You have to get ready for school!"

POP

As Scrizzie's vision cleared, he could see his mother's curly hair hanging over her left eye. He giggled.

"What's so funny, little boy?"

"You look like a pirate!" said Scrizzie.

"ARRRRRGH! A pirate, aye?" his mother said, giggling with him. "I'll shiver your timbers! Hurry and get ready for school, mate."

PLOP

Scrizzie, still giggly, threw back his blanket and hopped out of bed. He was so tickled that he didn't notice his big red fire engine in the middle of the floor and stumbled right over it.

"Oh, no!" he exclaimed, catching his balance—only to trip over his basketball and finally over his favorite sneakers and PLOP, down to the floor.

"Scrizzie, are you okay?" his mother asked.

"Yeah, I'm ok," Scrizzie answered, slowly getting up.

Scrizzie's mother looked puzzled. "Didn't I tell you to clean your room last night?"

"Uh, I did," replied Scrizzie quickly. He lowered his head and twiddled his thumbs, unable to look his mother in the eye.

"So how did it get like this?"

Scrizzie tried to think fast. Should he tell his mother the truth, or should he think of a clever way to stay out of trouble? Just as he was about to tell the truth he noticed the neighbors' dog, Mr. Ziggy, standing by his door. Scrizzie's family was dog-sitting Mr. Ziggy while the neighbors were on vacation.

Scrizzie blurted out, "It was Mr. Ziggy!" He could feel the heat spread across his face. In his heart Scrizzie knew he was not telling the truth.

"Well, if Mr. Ziggy created this much mess, we certainly can't dog-sit him again!" his mother said. She grabbed Mr. Ziggy by his collar and locked him in his pet carrier.

That wasn't the reaction Scrizzie expected from his mother. His heart sank as he looked at Mr. Ziggy's sad little face. Mr.Ziggy just wanted to walk Scrizzie to the bus stop and play fetch-the-stick. The little dog sighed and laid his head on his paws.

Scrizzie got ready for school, but he couldn't help thinking about Mr. Ziggy fastened in his pet carrier. Feeling guilty, Scrizzie stared out the window at the sky. To his surprise Zoomy was zooming toward him. "I sense that you aren't feeling very thankful today, Scrizzie."

"I'm not, Zoomy. I was dishonest with my mother and caused Mr. Ziggy to get in trouble." Scrizzie stared at his feet. "Now I will have to walk to my bus stop alone, and I can't play fetch-the-stick. I feel awful, Zoomy. I think I should tell the truth."

"Right you are, Scrizzie. If you tell the truth you will feel better, and so will Mr. Ziggy and your mother."

"Oh, Zoomy, you've bumped your head on an air wall again! My mom will be UPSET!"

Zoomy gave a gentle smile. "Sometimes telling the truth is very hard, Scrizzie, and your Mother WILL be disappointed. But she loves you and always wants you to make the right choices."

"I'm glad you've made the decision to confess. You will feel better about yourself and everyone else, Scrizzie," Zoomy said as he faded into the sky.

Scrizzie hurried down to breakfast, but before he sat down to eat he said, "Mom, I need to tell you the TRUTH about my room." His mother sat down at the table to listen to him. Scrizzie took a deep breath. "Mom, I apologize. I was disobedient. I did not clean my room. Worst of all I got Mr. Ziggy in trouble. I feel very sad."

Scrizzie's mother sighed. "I'm disappointed you did not tell me the truth, Scrizzie, and you let Mr. Ziggy take the blame for your messy room. But," she said, giving him a gentle hug, "I'm very pleased that you chose to confess, and I think Mr. Ziggy will be pleased also! Go let him out so you two can walk to the bus stop."

Scrizzie's face lit up with joy. He felt as light as a cloud as he zoomed down the hallway to free Mr. Ziggy.

Scrizzie's mother called after him, "You WILL clean your room after school—and NO playtime."

"Yes, Mom," Scrizzie said.

"Always remember, Scrizzie," she replied, "obedience is without sacrifice."

Scrizzie understood completely. If he had been obedient and cleaned his room he would not have to sacrifice his playtime. Scrizzie felt much better as he threw the stick and Mr. Ziggy fetched it. He looked up into the sky just as Zoomy zoomed by and winked. Scrizzie was happy, and so was Thankfulville.

THE END

CPSIA information can be obtained
at www.ICGtesting.com
Printed in the USA
LVIC06n1607110615
441828LV00004BB/5